IMAGES
of Wales

SWANSEA
1960s-1980s

An engraving done in 1880 showing Swansea at the zenith of its maritime-industrial powers.

IMAGES
of Wales

SWANSEA
1960s-1980s

Compiled by
City and County of Swansea

TEMPUS

First published 2002
Copyright © City and County of Swansea, 2002

Tempus Publishing Limited
The Mill, Brimscombe Port,
Stroud, Gloucestershire, GL5 2QG

ISBN 0 7524 2456 4

Typesetting and origination by
Tempus Publishing Limited
Printed in Great Britain by
Midway Colour Print, Wiltshire

Hafod schoolchildren on their garden plot in the lower Swansea valley, 1963.

Contents

Foreword

As we take our first steps into the new Millennium and contemplate the progress that is necessary for our city to develop, it seems an appropriate time to reflect on the changes that have already taken place. We all hold memories of how things used to be, but to try and explain to future generations how we saw things can sometimes be very difficult. So what better way to show what Swansea was like than through this wonderful pictorial record from the Council's Development Department. These photographs faithfully capture Swansea often on the cusp of change and span three decades, the 1960s, 1970s and 1980s. When we look back we will be able to see for ourselves the dramatic changes that have taken place in areas like the Lower Swansea Valley and Swansea Vale. To be able to see how once again our valley has been transformed from an area subsumed by heavy industry where nothing grew, to one that is now home to Europe's largest Urban Forest. In other parts of our City the changes have been just as dramatic. The old South Dock has been transformed into the award-winning Maritime Quarter. During this period we have also witnessed much change in our City Centre. In the 1960s we saw the new Swansea Market built and a new entrance into Swansea from the East created with the construction of the New Cut Bridge. The 1970s saw the Quadrant Shopping Centre, Leisure Centre and the Post Office Tower in the Strand, all changing the face of Swansea. The 1980s saw Britain's first Enterprise Zone designated in the Lower Swansea Valley. This book will bring back happy memories to many, and will be an Aladdin's Cave of pictorial wonder for those who want to discover the Swansea of yesteryear.

I am very grateful to Richard Porch of the City and County of Swansea's Development Department for his dedication in assembling such a marvelous pictorial record of a very important era in Swansea's history.

Councillor Byron G. Owen JP,
Cabinet Member for Development, City and County of Swansea

Introduction

By the middle of the twentieth century Swansea was already moving away from its heavy industrial heritage and beginning to acquire characteristics of the modern city we know today. It is fascinating to see, through these images, some of the changes actually taking place and astonishing to realise that they are all well within living memory.

Change to the environment is seldom recorded deliberately, often it is observed incidentally in the background of snapshots taken for other purposes. So it may come as a a surprise to discover that the Council's Development Services generate a large number of photographs in the course of their work. Such work is, in the main, executed by staff looking only to record for themselves this or that site prior to development. They are most often taken without the aid of a tripod and are often an over-the-shoulder kind of photography that owes nothing to the work of professional photographers. A small amount is commissioned from professionals but most is an amateur effort. Through area studies, individual planning applications and specific surveys the department has unwittingly created a remarkable visual record which now illustrates the changing face of the city and its districts. The greatest body of photography was done in the 1960s, '70s and '80s, when the city was going through its most dramatic period of change.

The book is divided into four chapters comprising the Maritime Quarter, City Centre, Swansea and District and the Lower Swansea Valley.

The Maritime Quarter: This area experienced the full cycle of history, enduring creation, success, failure and rebirth. Built between 1852-59 it was the engine room of Swansea's maritime-industrial success during the Industrial Revolution. By the end of the First World War the decline, which had already set in, accelerated during the depression years of the 1920s and '30s and later still by the disruption caused by the Second World War. The 1950s and '60s saw it fall, by degrees, into dereliction until the council stepped in to buy it, with redevelopment in mind, leading to the rebirth seen in the late 1970s.

The City Centre: Wartime bombing destroyed much of Swansea's city centre, most infamously, during the 'Three Nights Blitz' of 1941. Large tracts of the city were rebuilt in the 1950s and '60s, reorganizing the distribution of land use and providing wider streets that gave better access to cars. The sequence of photographs of Brynymor Road in 1970 shows a typical shopping street of the period and its shopfronts at the dawn of the age of the shopping centre and the superstore, servicing a car-borne customer. Pre-decimal prices, long-forgotten consumer goods and period graphics are all captured in this fascinating Area Study that also functions as a social document.

Swansea and District: This chapter looks at a variety of Swansea's districts ranging from Landore and Morriston to Sketty and Mumbles. There is a very professional-looking sequence of Mumbles, shot in the mid-1960s and capturing its inherently 'village' feel. In a nice touch, period saloon cars abound at a time when the price of petrol was measured in shillings per gallon rather than pounds per litre. This section looks particularly at ordinary streets of the period.

The Lower Swansea Valley (LSV): The LSV was once the largest area of industrial dereliction in Britain. It had its origins in the landscape reclamation project of the 1960s and a series of action plans published in the 1970s. These photographs were taken by Conservators at the very outset of the reclamation work and capture the harsh aridity and polluted nature of the LSV environment in the 1960s and '70s. The photography of the LSV is easily the most poignant in the book, and most of it is appears for the first time outside academic journals or textbooks. The project started in the early 1960s and has taxed the determination of successive generations of planners, councillors and academic colleagues at the University of Swansea. Forty years ago the Lower Swansea Valley was an arid and poisonous wasteland but now it is once more fit for human habitation and wildlife alike and is something we can all be proud of. Our valley is green once more.

Craig Anderson,
Director of Development, ARIBA, MRTPI.

Acknowledgements

One half of this book is composed of photographs taken by Council officers in the course of their duties, between 1960 and 1980. It would be a long and fruitless task to try and trace them all now. Suffice it to say we are grateful for the visual record of the City and County that they have unwittingly bequeathed to us.

The other half belongs to the University of Wales, Swansea, and the countless people involved in the Lower Swansea Valley Project that started in the early 1960s. We thank Professor D.T. Herbert and the Department of Geography for giving permission to use them.

I would also like to convey my appreciation to Katherine Burton, editor at Tempus Publishing, for her help and guidance and for enabling the compilation of this visual record to take place.

The photograph on p. 68 which shows Wern Road Chapel and the one on p. 99 of a lone person standing on a trial mound originally appeared in The Lower Swansea Valley Project, edited by K.J. Hilton, Longman, 1967.

Craig Anderson – Director of Development

One
Swansea Maritime Quarter

A view looking up the River Tawe at low tide during the late 1970s. Weaver's Flour Mill can still be seen and numerous boats sit on mudflats now rendered invisible by the barrage.

Unrecognizable under a thick coating of dereliction and builders' rubble, this is the award-winning Maritime Quarter in the late 1970s. In the middle of the photograph the Pumphouse stands, a derelict and forlorn shell, while the South Dock has been virtually filled in with debris. This view was taken from just outside the rear edge of what is now the Maritime Museum.

The rubble-strewn floor of the Tawe Basin at low tide, with the River Tawe beyond. This photograph was taken in the late 1970s.

This photograph dates from the early 1970s and was taken just in front of where the Maritime and Industrial Museum now is. It was a derelict shell when this photograph was taken. The museum building is just visible on the right. Looking beyond, only dockside sheds and rubble can be seen; County Hall has yet to be built.

This is a unique view obtained by standing in the South Dock when it was largely filled with builders' rubble in the late 1970s. The building beyond is the derelict Coastlines Warehouse, soon to be resurrected as the Maritime and Industrial Museum. Floating exhibits now occupy the space where this photograph was taken from.

The road on the right is now a car park behind the apartment blocks of Victoria Quay. The main entrance to the Maritime and Industrial Museum is at the centre of this mid-1970s photograph. The dramatic revetment walls on the left were built in the middle of the nineteenth century to carry an elevated railway into the heart of the docks. They were listed Grade II in March 1987.

This premises of Everwarm Homes Ltd at the County Hall end of the South Dock, sometime during the late 1970s.

The same view across the South Dock today would show the apartments on Victoria Quay. On the far right of this late 1970s photograph is the *Evening Post* building.

In the middle distance is the roof of what was to become the Maritime and Industrial Museum and the Pumphouse Restaurant beyond that. This early 1970s photograph seems to have been taken from cleared land where the Leisure Centre now stands.

Another unrepeatable photograph from the east side of the River Tawe, this time around 1981. The entrance to the South Dock is completely filled in with debris. In the centre of the picture the red-brick former Pumphouse and the Coastlines Warehouse lie derelict. Within a handful of years they would be refurbished as a steak restaurant and a museum respectively.

A work-in-progress photograph from the early 1970s showing landscaping under way around the South Dock, where the amphitheatre will later sit. The Coastlines Warehouse later to become the Maritime and Industrial Museum is dimly visible at the top of this murky photograph.

A still derelict Pumphouse and an intact swing bridge giving access to both sides of the South Dock in the late 1970s.

The Mannheim Quay residential development now stands where this photograph was taken, c. 1980. The view looks west towards Mumbles.

A lone oarsman in a very insubstantial-looking dinghy in the South Dock in the early 1970s.

An ex-Dutch coaster called *Schiestrom* is tied up alongside the South Dock in the early 1970s. The Pumphouse can clearly be seen in the middle-left foreground.

This photograph from the mid-1970s shows what is now called Pilot House Wharf. The building with the castellated tower was the Pilot House and can still be seen. The Barrage now occupies the middle of the picture and spans the Tawe at this point.

The trawler Lord Rodney is tied up at Pockett's Wharf in the mid-1970s.

The River Tawe in pre-barrage days, looking seaward, c. 1977. The castellated tower of the Pilot House can clearly be seen towards the top of the photograph. The extensive mudflats and the debris-strewn nature of the river at low tide are nicely demonstrated; all of this is now successfully hidden by the barrage.

The late Georgian terrace of Gloucester Place, attributed to the eighteenth-century Swansea architect, William Jernegan, seen here before restoration in the late 1980s.

Aerial view of Swansea's east side and its three operational docks in the 1970s. At the top left is the Prince of Wales Dock (1881), in the middle is the King's Dock (1909) and at far right is the Queen's Dock (1920).

This late 1970s view shows the mouth of the River Tawe at low tide with the King's Dock at the bottom of the picture and the Prince of Wales Dock just in view at bottom right. The entrance to the South Dock is at the top right.

Without lock-gates the Tawe Basin has dried out at low tide in this late 1970s view of what was later to become the award-winning Maritime Quarter docklands redevelopment. Access to the South Dock was impossible due to infilling. Weaver's Mill is still visible on the left.

The grand sweep of Swansea Bay is clearly visible in this view from the 1970s from Kilvey Hill. In the middle foreground the former docklands await redevelopment as the Maritime Quarter. Work is just starting on County Hall.

Two
The City Centre

The lych-gate of St Mary's church is seen here in the foreground as work gets underway on the new Quadrant Shopping Centre in 1976.

The Belle Vue Hotel before the building of the Quadrant Shopping Centre converted it into the Quadrant Gate during the late 1970s.

The Quadrant Shopping Centre replaced No. 22 Nelson Street in 1976.

Lower Union Street before the Quadrant Shopping centre was built, 1976. St Mary's church is clearly visible.

Oystermouth Road is here seen before the Leisure Centre footbridge was built; Oldway House is at the far left edge of this late 1970s photograph.

The big shed on the left belonged to City Electro Diesel Services in the late 1970s. It was the depot for the Mumbles train on Oystermouth Road.

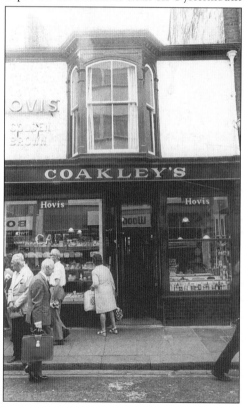

Coakley's bakers on Oxford Street in predecimal days, c. 1969.

This is Oxford Street twenty-five years ago, choked by lorries delivering goods to a Fine Fare supermarket. The Carlton Cinema is in the middle of the photograph.

This is a view from the mid-1970s looking west up Nelson Street. Clearly visible, four shop fronts along, is the entrance to the scene dock for the long-demolished Empire Theatre that fronted Oxford Street.

Nelson garages made way for the West Way in the mid-1970s.

Houses being demolished on the corner of Singleton Street in the late 1970s. The house still standing (on the right) survives today, as does the Singleton public house opposite.

The widening of the West Way called for the demolition of these houses on Dillwyn Street. The Grand Theatre before it was extended can be seen on the right in this view from the 1970s.

This shop, although not its blinds, is still there on the corner of Western Street and Argyle Street. The date of the photograph is around 1977.

The following sequence of twenty photographs of Brynymor Road was taken in 1970 and is a marvellous snapshot of a small shopping street just before the superstore and the shopping centre came to dominate the retail landscape completely. The two houses on the end housing Quiclean and Puddicombe's Meat Supply have been demolished but the rest remain. Although photographed nearly three-quarters of the way through the twentieth century, many original shop fronts can still be seen.

The Gloster Restaurant is now Monni's Fish Bar and Barry Hole has taken over from Billy Hole at the newsagents.

The Welsh Dry Cleaners is now part of the newsagents and Posie's the Florist is where Timothy White's used to be.

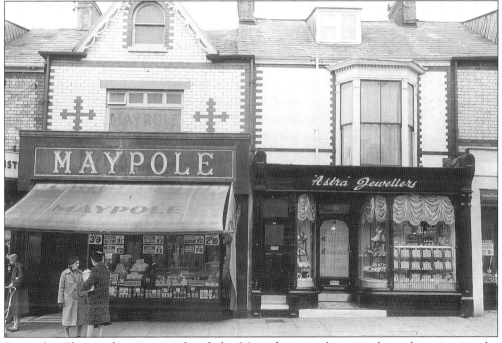

Boots the Chemist has since replaced the Maypole general store, where the prices in the window are still in shillings and pence. An Astra jewellers can still be found in the rear of the premises next door, while Diamond Cuts hairdressers occupies the front.

The Diecast Dreams toyshop is now where a quite modern-looking Country Maid shop was.

A vacant shop, formerly Ben Griffiths Weddings and Portraiture, is now the Lendart Laundrette. The Mary Morris dress shop is now vacant.

The once familiar Rentaset radio and TV hire shop is now the Vania Jesmond ladies' clothes shop, while Kandyland is now Sylvia's general store.

The Victoria Wine off-licence is now where Ernest Davies & Co. Ltd was. Remarkably, the Varsity Stores is still in the same location.

Watt's butchers shop is now Carroll's Catering Supplies.

E. Roberts, butchers, were selling Lincolnshire duckling at 3s 2d a pound when this photograph was taken. The John Bull Stores was where Travel Land travel agents is now.

The Brynymor Road post office was formerly a launderette and the Trustee Savings Bank is now Ferrari's baker shop.

Crundle's gift shop is now where H.B. King, the hardware store, used to be and Stephen Evans' opticians was formerly Gordon Cirel, men's outfitters.

In this view down Catherine Street the distant Guildhall clock tower says nearly 11.45 a.m.

Eynon's Pies café is now the Smokin' Dog bar and has become one bay smaller than in this photograph.

Bow's lingerie and swimwear shop can be found here now and Confectionery Supplies replaces Beryl Hurse's ladies' wear shop.

An ophthalmic optician is still at No. 72 Bryn y Mor Road, while the unnamed fruiterer's is now Swansea Packed Meals Chinese takeaway.

J.W. Harries is now the Brynymor House of Beauty, while H.M. Walters, the chemist and druggist, is now that most contemporary of retail outlets, the mobile phone shop.

Harrison's the wool shop and Johnson's dry cleaners shared the penultimate premises in Brynymor Road at this time. Today Brynymor Antiques and Collectables trades from here.

Glinsomoon's shop is now vacant.

Swansea Antique Centre now trades from the single-storey shops on the right. Perman's the fruiterers did so back in the 1990s.

A view from a disused railway bridge over Oystermouth Road in the early 1970s. The railway sleepers have already been pulled up on the right. They originally formed a network of sidings and tracks that fed the South Dock with coal from the valleys.

The Wales Gas compound on Oystermouth Road seen from near Bathurst Street in the early 1970s. In the middle distance is Swansea Market.

38

A view seen before the creation of the Quadrant and St David's shopping centres, from derelict land close to where the Leisure Centre now is. Swansea Market and St Mary's church can clearly be seen to the left and right. The hoardings at centre-right carry posters of Edward Heath, suggesting that this photograph was taken at some point during the General Election campaign of 1970.

The new College Street layout under construction, 7 February 1969.

A rare view of the Kingsway roundabout not encircled by cars, c. 1970.

New retail architecture meets old on Dillwyn Street in the mid-1970s.

Swansea Leisure Centre under construction in 1975-76.

The interior of the Palace Theatre in High Street. Built in 1888, this distinctive triangular building was converted into a cinema in 1908. By the time of this photograph, in the mid-1970s, it had metamorphosed for the final time into a bingo hall.

A picturesque view of the main façade of Swansea General Hospital, early 1980s.

An aerial view of Swansea city centre taken sometime in the early 1960s. Clearly visible is the Market, the derelict nature of the North Dock site and the former Castle Gardens.

Princess Way sometime in the mid-1970s. St Mary's church is on the right.

A view of Princess Way with St Mary's church, Boots and the rear of the Co-op, 22 December 1965.

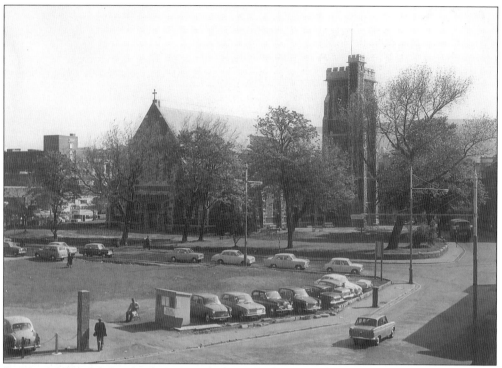

St Mary's church after landscaping, photographed from Rutland Street/Wassail Square on 6 June 1966. The surface parking in the foreground subsequently became a Littlewood's store.

A photograph taken in the late 1970s from near the lych-gate of St Mary's church. St David's Shopping Centre would be built upon the car parking area in the middle ground in 1982.

This marvellous Gothic-looking structure (actually built in 1912), was on Castle Bailey Street immediately adjacent to the *Evening Post* offices housed in the former post office (itself built in the 1850s). It was demolished in the 1970s.

This is a view from Caer Street in the late 1960s. The boarded-up building in the centre of this photograph is the old post office. It housed the offices of the *Evening Post* until 1968, when the newspaper moved to Adelaide Street.

Off-road parking when the *Evening Post* offices were located next to the Castle, late 1960s.

The thirteenth-century Swansea Castle stands surrounded by nineteenth-century additions in December 1967.

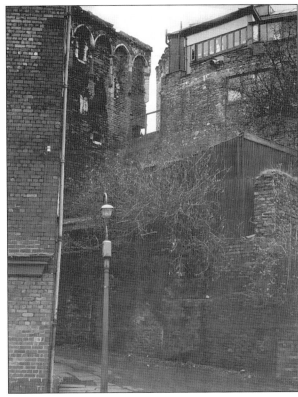

This is Castle Lane where it meets the Strand, c. 1969.

This panoramic view of Swansea's city centre was taken in the 1970s. Alexandra House on High Street is still under construction; at the top right of the picture Castle Square is still a garden and the post office stands next to the castle.

Castle Square in the mid-1970s, with the newly built Telecom Tower soaring futuristically above the ruins of Swansea Castle. The adjacent greetings card shop was demolished in the 1990s.

This run of three shops in Castle Square fell into dereliction and was demolished in the 1990s.

Paul's sold bathrooms when this photograph was taken in the mid-1970s. It now forms part of the Goose and Granite public house.

In the mid-1970s, the Duke public house and Roderick's clothes shop occupied Nos 2 and 3 Wind Street. They now form half of the Goose and Granite public house.

The Metropole Hotel in a state of dereliction on Wind Street during the mid-1970s.

The Tawe Boat and Swansea Sub-Aqua Clubs at the bottom of Wind Street in the middle 1970s.

J. Grinswell occupied this tight little niche in Wind Street's retail landscape. Both shop and adjacent railway abutments were demolished in the late 1970s.

The bottom of Wind Street again, this time showing the now demolished Green Shield Stamp showroom, c. 1978.

An atmospheric view of Salubrious Passage in Wind Street, c. 1979.

A far from Salubrious Passage in Wind Street, sometime before Easter in the 1970s. Munday's Wine Bar next door latterly became the No-Sign Wine Bar.

The changing face of pub design: the Pitcher and Piano bar has now replaced the Coach and Horses public house to be seen in this photograph of Wind Street from the late 1970s .

The Strand lined with vehicles sometime in the late 1970s.

The Telecom Tower in the Strand was started in the early 1970s and finished by 1975. It was re-clad in mirror-glass panels to great effect in the mid-1990s.

Weaver's Flourmill was built in 1897 and demolished in 1980. It was the first reinforced concrete building in Britain. A surviving beam from the mill can still be seen embedded in the ground near New Cut Bridge.

The Telecom Tower soaring in all its concrete glory over the Strand and Wind Street in the mid-1970s. Behind it lies the derelict land that twenty years hence would become the Parc Tawe retail development. High Street station can be seen in the middle-left foreground.

A rather sad-looking Somerset Place photographed well before restoration in the late 1970s. This distinctive little terrace dates from the late Georgian period (1820s) and is generally thought to be the work of Swansea's only Georgian architect, William Jernegan.

Three
Swansea and District

Dustbin day in Montana Row, Landore, in 1973. Brynhyfryd Baptist Chapel is top left.

A somewhat untidy-looking Montana Park, Landore in 1973.

A sunny Pwll Street, Landore, in 1973. The road is in much better shape today.

Hamilton Street, Landore, in 1973.

Pentre Hill in 1973. The Landore Viaduct is on the left and Cefn Hengoed School can be seen in the top right-hand corner.

The Tir John power station being demolished in 1976. It was opened in 1934 (the same year the Guildhall was completed) and closed in 1975.

The interior of the turbine hall of Tir John power station just prior to demolition in 1976.

This view across the Enterprise Park in the late 1970s appears to show that joyriding was not just a phenomenon of the 1990s.

Residents of Landore admire the quality of work involved in forming this parking bay in the mid-1970s.

A solitary thinker sits outside the Dyfatty flats in 1973.

The Bonymaen Stone, landscaped by volunteers in 1974.

A deserted Davis Street playground in Plasmarl, February 1977.

Fagwr Place playground in Morriston during February 1977. The walling in this photograph, particularly to the left-hand side, shows much use of slag blocks.

A 'before' photograph of a rather grim looking playground in a General Improvement Area, Port Tennant, 1975.

Taking the sun: a photograph taken in Port Tennant in 1975.

The Joseph Davies Close development at Waun Wen, 1960s. In the background is some pre-war housing at Townhill.

The Blaen-y-Maes Ravine seen from the air, prior to landscaping works in the 1970s.

An old car dumped in Blaen-y-Maes, 1970.

Lark Place in Blaen-y-Maes, 12 April 1973. Demolishing older derelict housing created the gentle hillocks; the scrub and elm trees were retained.

Heading home with the shopping on a spring afternoon in Blaen-y-Maes during the mid-1970s.

Wern Road Chapel is on the left, Landore station is in the middle and some new council housing can be seen at middle-left, 1963.

Post-war council housing in West Cross, late 1970s.

Swansea foreshore at West Cross on a summer's evening in 1960.

The Halfway Garage is at left-centre of this photograph taken in the mid-1960s. Note the street lamps made from converted tram power line supports.

An empty No. 74 bus (Sketty, Uplands and High Street station) skirts a brand new petrol station in Sketty. The flat roofs of Parklands School can be seen to the left of it. The garage has long since disappeared to make way for sheltered housing and the Spinning Wheel public house is now on the left. The date is sometime in the mid-1960s.

The Tivoli when it was still a cinema and a dance hall in the mid-1960s. Hilary Amis, the ex-wife of the novelist Sir Kingsley Amis, worked at the Tivoli in the early 1960s. The small building on the end, next to the Castle Garage, was a police box.

The Tivoli is on the left, the Castle Garage is in the middle and the tennis courts are to the right of the police box. The truncated traffic light on the post notified the bobby on the beat to call the station in the days before two-way radios. These were introduced in 1965, which dates this Mumbles picture to the early 1960s.

A.D. Lloyd of Blackpill Garage taking a delivery of petrol, *c.* 1964.

The domestic scale of life in Mumbles in the mid-sixties is nicely captured in this photograph of William Pressdee, funeral director and supplier of 'Cars for all Occasions'. Next door is W.S. Davies, painter and decorator.

Besides showing some classic saloon cars of the mid-sixties, this photograph shows Ted Priddy the hairdresser's, formerly Ernie Venton's the cobbler's. Eric J. Owen's garage and cycle shop is next to Oakley Peachey's general store.

Oakley Peachey's general store selling best King Edward new potatoes at 1s per pound around 1964-65. Further along Eric J. Owen's garage was formerly Peachey's livery stables.

Austin A40s abound in this photograph, when the price of BP Super was 4s 10d a gallon. The garage belonged to J.L. Ace and it was opposite the Rock and Fountain public house in Newton Road. The date is around 1964.

The Davies, Roe & Muxworthy Ltd car showroom in Sketty, mid-1960s.

Croft Garage, at the bottom of Cockett Road, on a winter's day in the mid-1960s.

A quiet day at the pumps in around 1964 allows the proprietor of this Mumbles petrol station to pop across to the tobacconists.

A petrol station on Derwen Fawr Road in the mid-1960s when all they sold was petrol and spare parts.

Blackpill Lido in Mumbles, a good thirty years before its refurbishment.

The compact scale of Woodfield Street in Morriston is nicely captured here in the late 1970s.

Radio Rentals and Calnic Electrical Repairs feature in this run of shops on Woodfield Street.

The face of shopping changes forever as purpose-built parades of shops begin to replace converted Victorian housing. This is Woodfield Street between 1965 and 1969.

At the far left in the window of Evans Auto, tyres are for sale at 75s each!

The traditional shop fronts of Phillips' Radio and S.W. Jewellers stand out in this run of shops of thirty years ago.

Old housing meets new in this view from the late 1960s of the Strand, Cwmfelin. The Victorian terrace at right still has many of its original features such as sash windows, timber doorcases and Welsh slate roofs.

A branch of Eynon's bakeries occupies this site next to the Card Gallery. Lots of little details allow us to date this photograph. The design of the television aerials, slate roofs, the preponderance of timber sash windows and the lamp standard made from an old tram power line support, all place this firmly in the late 1960s.

Woodfield Street at the junction with Crown Street.

R.C. Greep is the ironmongers seen in the middle in the late 1960s.

The clock high on the wall above Munday's wine merchants says 10.50 a.m.

A marvellous stepped cascade of Victorian shop fronts acts as a backdrop for the 'pop van' calling at E.G. Hopkins, in the late 1960s.

The relentless march of modern shop fronst through a typical late-Victorian shopping street has here been nicely caught in Morriston, where Slate Street meets Woodfield Street, c. 1969.

One thing is for sure: there were no expensive trail bikes in the window of L.E.D. Davies on this summers morning in Morriston, in the late 1960s. In those far-off days cyclists could still be found riding in the road and usually had to possess a cycling proficiency test before being allowed out on the highway.

This CRS Supermarket was offering 'Dividend Double Stamps'. Trading stamps were an early form of the modern loyalty card popular in the 1960s and '70s. In the window, boxes of Daz washing powder were selling for 2s 11d and tinned pears for 1s 9d. Decimal currency was introduced in 1971.

Purpose-built shops arrive on Woodfield Street in the mid-1960s, in the form of this Peglers Supermarket. Inside were beans for 1s per tin, tea at 1s 4d a packet, a tin of Nestlé cream was 1s 1d and cigarettes were 3s for twenty.

In the middle 1960s you could find Albany Furnishers and D.W. Jones near the corner of Cwm Bath Road.

The distinctive half-timbered look of the Crown Inn and its turret catch the eye in this photograph of Woodfield Street in the late 1960s.

Four

The Lower Swansea Valley

A cold winter's day at the river weir in the early 1960s. In the middle of the photograph is the huge tapered stone chimney of the Morfa Silverworks, which was demolished in 1969. Kilvey Hill is to the right.

At low tide the remains of many timber features could be seen in the river. Log pilings that ships rested on while tied up, former lockgates and jetties could all be seen.

A view across to Pentre Guinea Road from land next to New Cut Road in October 1975.

When this photograph was taken in October 1976 at Foxhole, riverside improvements and landscaping were still some way off.

The railway line that was in place at Foxhole in October 1976 is now a cycle path. The copper workers' place of worship, All Saints Church, is just out of view at top right.

Two views of the Beaufort Tip (Cohen's) taken in 1963 and 1976 respectively. Above is a vast slag heap forming a veritable cliff edge of waste material reaching almost to the water's edge. Below, fourteen years later, the slow but sure pace of renewal has seen the removal of the tip and the next phase of the clean-up could begin.

Track repairs were being carried out at Foxhole during the mid-1960s. Notice the slag block coping stones on the bridge parapet in the left-hand corner of this photograph.

This was taken sometime in the mid-sixties and in a frighteningly arid landscape, the fly tipping of builders' rubble begins to create another tip, somewhere in the lower Swansea valley.

The British Steel slag tip, near Siemens' laboratory in 1963. Morris Castle is on the skyline at the far left and extensive fly tipping is adding to the sense of dereliction.

Wagon tipping on an established slag heap, 1963. The Fendrod stream wends its way through a marshy lagoon of possibly toxic waste. The 'bumps' in the foreground were caused by zinc waste. Morris Castle can just be made out above the wagons.

A very long-range view taken from the opposite side of the valley, looking towards White Rock tip during clearance work in 1970.

A 1965 view over the Morfa copper works tip. The Landore Viaduct bisects the photograph and Morris Castle can be seen on the skyline. The 'For Sale' signs are up on many acres of slag and derelict industrial buildings.

The view at the end of Aberdyberthi Street in Hafod, in 1963. Visible at the end of the street is the Pentre-Hafod tip that was made of slag from the Vivian works and covered five hectares. The first tip removal project in the valley started here in 1967 and cost over £400,000.

Boulders of fused slag (slag that has merged when still hot) and builders' rubble litter the foreground, looking towards Landore in the 1970s.

A late 1960s view across the River Tawe at low tide, to the Yorkshire Imperial Metals site. The main Swansea to London railway line can be seen slicing through a landscape littered with slag heaps and dereliction.

This view was taken from Kilvey Hill, overlooking the Addis works, in 1976. On the skyline are the ruins of Morris castle, built in the 1770s for John Morris I to house his employees. In the middle distance is the Landore Viaduct, originally designed by Isambard Kingdom Brunel between 1847 and 1850. Spanning the Tawe below that is a 1909 bascule bridge, a rare surviving example of a counterpoised lifting bridge. The Morfa Stadium and playing fields have yet to be created.

The River Tawe passing through a ravaged landscape near where the Morfa Stadium is now, in the mid-1970s.

The Rio Tinto zinc and sulphuric acid plant in August 1974. It had closed a month earlier.

This landscape looks like something from a science fiction film; it is in fact the ICI tip in 1962.

An atmospheric view looking through what looks like the arch of some long-demolished bridge. This view looks toward Cwm School in 1975.

Two views of the Morganite site before construction took place in the mid-1960s. A considerable amount of the White Rock tip was broken up and used to raise and level the site ready for development.

This is the Llansamlet copper and arsenic works in 1964-65. Units of the local Territorial Army later demolished the stacks using explosives. Note the line of railway buffers in the middle ground, showing how railway lines were laid over an existing slag heap.

The road at the right is Cwmlan Terrace and the truck belongs to Eddie Jenkins who had a house and stables at bottom right (out of sight). Just visible ,at centre-right alongside the telegraph pole, is parked one of the horse-drawn carts used for collecting ashes. The date is sometimes in the early 1960s.

A classic image from the early 1960s, taken somewhere in the Lower Swansea Valley. Fly-tipped material and boulders of fused slag abound in this poisoned landscape.

The surviving remains of the Siemens works laboratory building in 1963. The Landore viaduct looms into view at bottom right.

It is sometime in the mid-1960s and a lone visitor (probably a Conservator) stands on a trial mound where young trees have been planted. The site was once the Llansamlet copper and arsenic works.

Pluck Lake is on the right and the chimney belongs to the Llansamlet copper and arsenic works. The tractor driver is ploughing the soil to turn it over as an aid to reclamation and later seeding. The date is around 1962.

This smoky view from 1963 looks east across the valley from Trewyddfa Road towards Cwm and Bonymaen.

Youngsters play near the Vale works in the mid-1960s. The stone ruins to the right were part of an old colliery below Cwm.

Territorial Army officers inspect the former Llansamlet Copper and Arsenic works in May 1963. The stack behind them was later demolished with explosives.

The landscaping of the sites of former slag heaps was already under way when this photograph was taken in 1963. However, the grim aridity of the valley prior to reclamation was still all too visible.

Kilvey Hill in the late 1960s. The Pentre Guinea Road bisects the picture diagonally and the grey mass of the Hafod Tip can still be seen in the upper-middle half of this picture.

This view was taken from the top of a slag heap on the White Rock side of the river and shows the derelict Yorkshire Imperial Metals works in 1963. About the only features that still survive are the clock tower of the canteen block, just visible at the dead centre of the photograph and the two chimneys at left.

This photograph was taken in 1974 from a position opposite the White Rock site and on a former railway line that fed the Vivian engine shed. The building opposite has now largely disappeared.

The Landore Viaduct crossing the River Tawe in the early 1960s.

The same view roughly ten years later, in 1975, looking south down the River Tawe.

These two views show some of the fascinating industrial archaeology to be found among the spoil heaps and ruins in 1963.

Here and there among the drifts of slag, all manner of architectural features occasionally broke through, most of them probably of lost Victorian.

The land at the very bottom of this picture from 1963 became the site of the Morganite works. The gas holder survives to this day, while virtually everything else has been landscaped and built upon afresh.

Looking north this time from the same view point and at the same date. The northern reaches of what was to become the Enterprise Zone were still hideously disfigured by slag heaps and derelict factories.

Taken at some point in the early 1960s, this photograph shows what was to become the Enterprise Park at Clase Road, before Morganite was built. Derelict land, the ruins of former factories, surviving industrial concerns and a landscape exhausted by continuous industrialization over two centuries can all be seen in this picture.

Morganite Electrical Carbon Ltd was one of the first industrial concerns to set up in the lower Swansea valley in the 1960s. This photograph was taken in the mid-1970s, when the quality of the surrounding environment had already improved greatly.

The gas holder at the bottom left is still there and the curious earthwork in the middle of the photograph hides a scrapyard. This was the Enterprise Park at Ferryboat Close in 1978.

The Swansea to London railway line sweeps off the floor of the valley and into the city. In this late 1970s photograph the site of the future Morfa Stadium has yet to be cleared and landscaped ready for development.

The Landore Viaduct snakes out of view on the left-hand side of this picture. In the middle is the British Steel Corporation's Landore plant and the 'Half-Round Pond' (still to be seen today) is sandwiched between two large slag heaps.

This vast slag heap near British Steel Landore dwarfed everything around it, seen here in the late 1970s. Even a lagoon is forming (bottom left).

The saw-tooth shaped roof of the Addis works can be seen top left. At the top right is the Landore Viaduct and at middle right is Pluck Lake. Railway lines feature prominently in this late 1970s photograph.

High above the Addis works on the River Tawe, the land where the Morfa Stadium now stands has yet to be recovered from the slag heaps. The Landore viaduct bisects the middle of this picture.

Aerial view from March 1977 showing the A48 and the entrance to the Rio Tinto zinc works. The road running horizontally across the picture is now Bran Close.

The London to Swansea railway line crosses the River Tawe near the British Steel Corporation's plant at Landore in March 1977. Clearly visible in this picture is the embanking at the eastern end of the Landore viaduct, a later modification to Brunel's original design of 1847-50.

Here are the remains of the Yorkshire Imperial Metals works in March 1977. Only the canteen block with its clock tower (centre top of photograph) and two chimneys down near the river still survive.

A lone fisherman on the River Tawe at Morriston, probably near Beaufort Reach, in 1975. The rampant undergrowth all around him is none other than Fallopia japonica, the ubiquitous 'Japanese Knotweed'.

Two successful fishermen at Beaufort Bridge on the River Tawe at Morriston in 1975. The 'catch' is probably either trout or sewin.

Competitors and spectators gather in a car park near the base of the ski slope for a cross-country cycle race in October 1976. The 'cutting' to the rear is now Nantong Way.

A school party gets a lesson in scything long grass in September 1964. Lower Swansea Valley Project staff began giving lectures to children during school hours, as early as 1962. The involvement of the young in tree planting and maintenance project work was seen as vital to giving them a sense of 'ownership' of the project.

Schoolchildren from Plasmarl on a tree-planting expedition in 1963.

These Plasmarl schoolchildren posed for this photograph while they were being given a talk on the range of trees they were going to be planting on their school plot. They were silver birch, common alder, Japanese larch, black locust, hornbeam, red oak, sitka spruce, elm, grey alder and London plane.

This is perhaps the most appealing of all the lower Swansea valley photographs as well as being the most self-consciously 'posed'. Here a mixed group of primary schoolchildren plant trees in the Hafod School plot in 1963.

Here among some revegetated slag heaps some schoolchildren plant trees on the Hafod School plot in 1966. In the background a newly landscaped slag mound still has some fused material protruding from it at top right. To the left of that, some redundant machinery still towers into the sky, while right on the horizon the Cefn Hengoed School is dimly visible. They are planting rhododendrons. The large shovel-like implement being held by one girl is a rubber fire-beater.

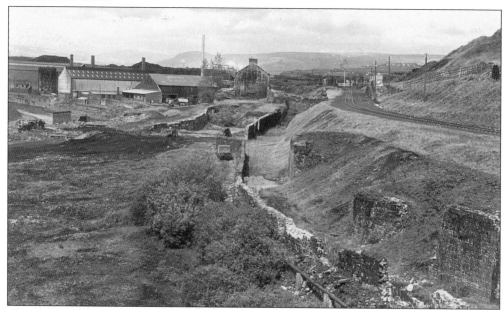

The cluster of buildings at top left is now the Addis Works. The remains of Smith's canal, built between 1783 and 1785, snakes away from the right-hand corner to the centre of this picture taken in 1965. What remained of the canal was filled in and the railway line at top right became a road. The whole area has been successfully landscaped and declared an area of archaeological interest.

This view looks back toward the city centre down the line of Smith's canal in 1965. The bulldozers belong to the local Territorial Army Engineers who used the exercise to hone their skills in demolition and clearance.

Plainly visible in this 1963 view are some of the eighteenth-century remains of the White Rock Copperworks that were soon to be demolished due to their unsafe condition. In the background loom other slag heaps and one vast slag boulder.

The White Rock site was on the way to being flattened in 1963. Every standing structure was razed, save the large shed at the centre, the remains of which can still be seen today. The River Tawe was at low tide and is out of picture on the far right.

The levelled ruins of the White Rock copper works can be seen on the right in 1963. Clearly visible also is a Victorian quay that has collapsed into the River Tawe. Judging from the tracks left by former railway lines in the foreground, this photograph was taken from near the Vivian engine sheds. On the other side of the river can be seen the stacks of the Hafod copper works, which was active between 1810-1924.

A lone bus skirts the flattened White Rock copper works in 1976. In the foreground are the remains of an early quay and dock used for the unloading of coal or copper ore. The whole site was designated the White Rock Industrial Archaeological Park in the 1980s.

This view from 1963 looking down the River Tawe towards the sea can still be seen today, although the landing stage at middle-right has gone, as have the stone buildings at middle-left. General landscaping and riverside improvements have returned this view to something like the way it might have looked 250 years ago.

The Territorial Army flattens a tip at White Rock in 1962. On the other side of the river are the derelict engine sheds of Vivian and Sons. The imprint of former railway tracks is clearly visible, as are the towering slag heaps at the top of the photograph.

The Vivian and Sons' engine shed overlooking the Tawe, opposite White Rock, 1963. The walls were made from Vivian's own 'patent' brick, a type based on crushed slag.

The River Tawe at Morriston in 1975. The pinnacle of Morriston Tabernacle can just be seen clearing the undergrowth lining the river.

At the far left can be seen Pluck Lake crowded in on all sides by slag heaps, 1965. In the foreground a young plantation of trees has been started.

The British Steel works on the Tawe in 1975.

The Swansea Canal near Landore/Glandwr in 1963. In 1931 the last working Swansea canal boat with man and horse had worked this canal. Behind the sign to the works can be seen the soaring stack of the Morfa Silverworks which was demolished approximately six years later.

A walk among the ruins of the Llansamlet copper and arsenic works in 1962. This is a southward view towards the city centre and the sea.

Twelve years later, in 1974, this is what that same site looked like after landscaping and revegetation.

A diesel train (No. 08658), pulling goods wagons, passes close by Pluck Lake, 1963. This is now Nantong Way linking the Enterprise Park to the cross-valley link at the tennis centre.

This is the White Rock Works in dereliction in 1975. Derelict buildings, the debris caused by the fly-tipping of household waste and the remnants of slag heaps are still all too prominent.

This view looks west across what is now the Enterprise Zone in 1963.

This is a view of the former Upper Forrest and Worcester Works at Morriston on 13 April 1967. Levelling and site clearance were shortly to start. This view looks south-west from the northern part of the site.

Magnificently anonymous in its scale, colour this photograph red and you could be on the planet Mars. It was part of the White Rock Tip in 1963.

The Llansamlet/Worcester Works, photographed from Trewyddfa Road in 1963. At the far left is the so-called 'cathedral of Welsh non-conformity', Morriston Tabernacle.

The main London to Swansea railway line cuts through the centre of this 1968 view. Pluck Lake glistens at the centre of the image, while above it (and on the other side of the river) sit the remains of the Hafod Works.

This aerial view of the valley floor gives some idea of the scale of the dereliction in 1963. The Fendrod stream meanders crookedly through the bottom half of the picture, the half-round pond is just visible at middle-right. Nowadays the Wyevale Garden Centre and Jaguar showroom share the middle-left foreground with the Fendrod Lake.

Even high on Kilvey Hill overlooking White Rock, it was the slag heaps that dominated the landscape of this photograph from 1963.

It is 1968 and a house-sized boulder of fused slag over looks the traffic in this photograph of Kilvey Hill above the White Rock Copper Works.